THE POWER OF VISION
OFFICIAL WORKBOOK

CHARTING YOUR SPIRITUAL COURSE

MARK COWART

Harrison
House

Harrison House P.O. Box 310, Shippensburg, PA 17257-0310

This book and all other Harrison House's books are available at Christian bookstores and distributors worldwide.

For Worldwide Distribution.

Reach us on the Internet: www.harrisonhouse.com.

ISBN 13 TP: 9781667510354

ISBN 13 eBook: 9781667510361

CONTENTS

INTRODUCTION

Welcome to *The Power of Vision Official Workbook*, a journey that will challenge, inspire, and equip you to unlock God's heavenly vision for your life, community, and nation. The vision God has for you is not small or insignificant; it is a divine blueprint designed to guide you into a life of purpose, victory, and eternal significance. Through the pages of this workbook, we will explore foundational biblical principles, real-life applications, and the spiritual strategies needed to embrace and walk in the vision God has placed within you.

The Power of Vision is more than just a concept; it is a spiritual reality rooted in God's Word. Throughout the chapters ahead, you will see how God uses vision to guide, correct, and empower His people. As you engage with the teachings, you will discover that vision is a dynamic force that shapes your future, strengthens your faith, and aligns your life with God's purposes. Vision gives direction to the dream God placed inside of you, and this workbook will help you take practical steps to see it come to fruition.

From the very beginning, you will be reminded that **your vision must align with God's Word**. Scripture is the bedrock upon which all true vision is built. When we understand that the Bible is God's revealed will for humanity, we realize that any heavenly vision will never contradict His Word. You will learn to take your thoughts captive, guard your heart, and allow God's truth to become the foundation for your life. Without the Word of God, vision can be hijacked by the enemy, distracted by the world, or weakened by fear. But with the Word as your anchor, your vision will remain steadfast.

One of the key themes woven throughout this workbook is that **testing plays a significant role in the fulfillment of God's vision**. Tests, trials, and adversity are not to be feared or avoided but embraced as opportunities for growth and preparation. James 1:3 reminds us, "The testing of your faith produces patience." God uses seasons of testing to refine our character, deepen our trust in Him, and prepare us for the responsibilities that come with fulfilling His vision. Just as Jesus faced the ultimate test in the Garden of Gethsemane before fulfilling His mission at the cross, we too must endure tests that strengthen our resolve and obedience.

Throughout these chapters, you will see that **the power of imagination is key to realizing the vision God has given you.** Your imagination is not merely a tool for creativity; it is a divine gift that allows you to see possibilities beyond your current circumstances. Vision begins with seeing—through your spiritual eyes—the future God has planned for you. You will learn to reject limiting beliefs, take hold of God's promises, and dream big dreams inspired by the Holy Spirit. Just as Joseph's God-given dreams propelled him into his destiny, so too can your dreams become the catalyst for fulfilling God's vision in your life.

Another critical takeaway from this workbook is the importance of **obedience and faithfulness in stewarding your**

vision. Vision without action is meaningless. God requires us to be faithful with the little before He entrusts us with more. You will see how obedience—even in the face of adversity—leads to breakthrough and favor. King Saul's failure to obey God's instructions cost him his kingdom, but Joseph's unwavering faithfulness in every season, from the pit to the palace, led to his exaltation and the fulfillment of his God-ordained purpose.

In addition to personal application, this workbook will encourage you to see **the broader purpose of vision within your community and nation.** America, as a modern-day manifestation of the heavenly vision, serves as a powerful reminder of what is possible when a people seek first the Kingdom of God. You will explore how biblical principles formed the foundation of this nation and how a return to those principles is essential for its future. The challenges we face today—spiritual decline, moral compromise, and cultural confusion—are not insurmountable when viewed through the lens of God's vision. You are called to be a light in the darkness, to stand for truth, and to pray for revival in your land.

The **importance of righteous leadership** is another recurring theme in this workbook. Whether you lead a family, a business, a ministry, or simply influence those around you, your leadership matters. Leaders who are guided by God's vision bring hope, direction, and transformation to those they serve. You will be encouraged to embrace a servant-leader approach, modeled by Jesus Christ Himself, who came "not to be served, but to serve" (Mark 10:45). Leadership requires humility, boldness, and an unwavering commitment to God's purposes.

This workbook also emphasizes the role of **godly relationships in fulfilling your vision.** God never intended for you to walk this journey alone. He will align you with people whose hearts are stirred toward the same heavenly goals. Relationships that are divinely ordained will strengthen your faith, multiply your resources, and help you accomplish what you could never do alone. You will also learn to guard against relationships that hinder your progress and distract you from God's calling.

As you move through these pages, you will repeatedly be reminded that **vision requires perseverance.** Challenges will come, and the enemy will attempt to derail you through fear, doubt, and distraction. But the truth remains: **light always overcomes darkness.** No opposition, no adversity, and no weapon formed against you can stop God's vision from coming to pass when you remain steadfast. Philippians 4:13 declares, "I can do all things through Christ who strengthens me."

Lastly, this workbook will challenge you to **see yourself as part of the Great Commission**—the heavenly vision that calls every believer to take the Gospel to the ends of the earth. You are not only called to receive vision but to share it with others. God has given you unique gifts, talents, and resources that He intends for you to use to advance His Kingdom. Your vision is not just about personal success; it is about making an eternal impact.

By the time you complete this workbook, my prayer is that you will have a deeper understanding of God's vision for your life and the courage to pursue it with all your heart. You will be equipped with biblical truths, practical steps, and spiritual strategies to overcome obstacles and walk in victory. Whether you are facing tests, seeking clarity, or striving to fulfill a long-held dream, **this workbook will help you take hold of God's promises and walk in His divine purpose.**

God is not finished with you. He is not finished with your family, your ministry, or your nation. The power of vision is alive, and it is waiting for you to embrace it. Let us rise to the challenge, seek first His Kingdom, and become Kingdom disciples who run with the heavenly vision. Together, we will see His glory revealed, His plans fulfilled, and His light shine brightly in every area of our lives.

"Where there is no vision, the people perish: but he that keepeth the law, happy is he."

—Proverbs 29:18 KJV

Let's begin this journey together. It is time to discover, develop, and deploy the vision God has placed within you.

~

CHAPTER I

LOGOS VS. RHEMA

"Your word I have hidden in my heart, That I might not sin against You." - Psalm 119:11 NKJV

I n writing this chapter, my journey began out of a deep sense of **Vision Through Desperation**. Back in 1987, as a newly appointed senior pastor, I found myself at the helm of a church grappling with immense challenges. This personal trial led me to delve into the study of vision, not merely as an academic exercise, but as a lifeline. I discovered that often, it is through our greatest trials that God molds our greatest insights.

Reflecting on this period, I realized a profound truth that God does not call the equipped but rather, **God Equips the Called**. This revelation came at a time when my wife and I, in our late twenties, felt wholly inadequate to lead a struggling congregation. Yet, it was during these formative years that we experienced firsthand how God prepares those He has chosen, providing not just spiritual but also practical leadership skills when they are most needed.

Throughout my early days in ministry, the significance of

having mentors became abundantly clear. Influential figures like Peter Daniels and Dr. Lester Sumrall played pivotal roles in shaping my understanding of spiritual leadership. Daniels, a successful entrepreneur despite his disadvantaged background, and Dr. Sumrall, with his vast ministry experience, both exemplified how **Impact of Leadership Mentors** can profoundly influence one's path. They taught me that leadership is not just about guiding others but also about continuously growing and adapting oneself.

Dr. Sumrall once shared an insightful view on life's progression, describing it as divided into **Three Trimesters of Life**. He explained that the first thirty years are for absorbing knowledge, the next thirty are for building upon that knowledge, and the last thirty are for giving back. This framework has guided me in structuring my life and ministry, emphasizing that each phase has its unique purpose and contribution to one's overall life mission.

One of the most critical insights I have gained in my ministry relates to the distinction between **Logos vs. Rhema**. The logos, or the written Word of God, and rhema, the revealed or spoken Word, serve different but complementary purposes in our spiritual lives. Understanding this distinction has been key to unlocking the transformative power of the scriptures. The logos provides a solid foundation of knowledge, while the rhema personalizes and activates this knowledge in applicable and dynamic ways.

This distinction became vividly real to me through a personal experience that underscored the importance of **Spiritual Warfare and the Rhema Word**. I encountered demonic forces that were dispelled by the power of the rhema Word, a moment that not only strengthened my faith but also demonstrated the practical application of God's Word in spiritual warfare.

The **Role of the Word in Spiritual Identity** was particularly highlighted during the temptation of Jesus in the wilderness, where He countered Satan's attacks with specific scriptures. This episode illustrates how the rhema Word serves as our spiritual sword, defending our identity in Christ against the enemy's deceptions.

My reflection on spiritual growth also led me to understand the dangers posed by our **Appetites and Spiritual Deception**. Just as Adam and Eve were led astray by a seemingly innocent desire, we too are often tempted to fulfill legitimate needs through illegitimate means. Recognizing and controlling our appetites is crucial in maintaining spiritual integrity and focus.

Moreover, I have come to see that every believer is called into ministry, regardless of their professional or social status. **Ministerial Call to All Believers** is a profound truth that underscores the universal calling to serve God and advance His kingdom. This understanding should empower every Christian to live out their faith actively, knowing they are anointed to function in both priestly and kingly capacities.

Lastly, the pursuit of God's vision for our lives requires steadfastness and endurance. **Perseverance in Pursuit of Vision** is essential, as the journey is often met with opposition. However, the rewards—both temporal and eternal—are immense for those who diligently seek and fulfill God's purposes.

Reflective Questions

1. How has a period of hardship or pressure in your own life led you to seek deeper spiritual truths or insights?
2. In what ways have you experienced God equipping you for tasks or roles you felt unprepared for?
3. Who are the mentors in your life who have influenced

your spiritual growth, and what key lessons have you learned from them?

4. How do you currently align your life's phases—learning, building, giving back—with the biblical understanding of growth and maturity?

5. Can you identify moments when the Word of God became 'rhema' to you, transforming your understanding or approach to a situation?

ACTIONABLE STEPS

- **Cultivate a Visionary Mindset**: Begin a daily practice of journaling your visions and insights as you study the Word of God. This will help you to identify and clarify the specific 'rhema' that God is speaking into your life.
- **Equip with Knowledge:** Commit to a structured Bible study plan that focuses on the distinction between logos and rhema. This will equip you with the theological understanding necessary to discern and apply the Word more effectively in your life.
- **Engage in Spiritual Warfare**: Regularly practice declaring the 'rhema' Word over your life situations, especially during times of spiritual warfare. This active engagement with the Word will strengthen your spiritual identity and authority.

JOURNALING **Prompt**

Reflect on a recent situation where you experienced a 'rhema' moment—where something you read in the Bible suddenly became very clear or directly applicable to a circumstance in your life. What was the scripture, and how did it change your perspective or action in that situation?

~

CHAPTER 2
WHAT IS VISION?

"Where there is no vision, the people perish: but he that keepeth the law, happy is he." —Proverbs 29:18 KJV

In this exploration of **Vision**, we dive deep into its significance, far beyond the ordinary definitions found in dictionaries. Vision encompasses not just the physical act of seeing but involves the profound ability to perceive spiritual realities and foresee the possibilities that faith in God opens up to us. When we discuss vision in a biblical context, we are indeed talking about the capacity to see beyond the natural—to envision what is not yet visible to the physical eye.

It's critical to recognize that we have been delivered from **spiritual blindness**, a condition far more debilitating than physical blindness. This concept was powerfully illustrated in the transformation of Saul, who encountered Jesus on the road to Damascus. His physical and spiritual sight were restored, symbolizing the enlightenment that comes from an encounter with Christ. This moment of transformation marks a profound realization of our inheritance in Christ—of all that Jesus has purchased for us through His sacrifice. This inheritance is not just a future promise but a present reality, meant to impact how we live today.

The scriptures enrich our understanding by revealing that we possess **two sets of eyes**—one that sees the physical world and another that perceives spiritual truths. The Old Testament story of Elisha and his servant vividly illustrates this. Surrounded by an enemy army, the servant was consumed by fear until his spiritual eyes were opened, revealing the divine protection surrounding them. This moment underscores the essence of spiritual vision, transforming fear into faith when we see with our spiritual eyes.

When **Elisha prayed for his servant's eyes to be opened**, it wasn't just for the young man to see the angelic forces; it was a plea for him to perceive God's power and presence, which are always near, though often invisible to our physical eyes. This spiritual perception is essential, for it is what allows us to live by faith, not by sight, trusting in God's protection and provision even when they are not apparent to our physical senses.

In the New Testament, **Paul's ministry** further emphasizes the importance of spiritual sight. Standing before King Agrippa, Paul articulated his divine mission to open the eyes of the Gentiles, turning them from darkness to light—from the power of Satan to God. This transition enables us to receive the forgiveness of sins and step into the inheritance God has prepared for us, illuminating our spiritual destiny.

The danger of **blinded minds**, as discussed by Paul, is particularly poignant. Such blindness prevents people from seeing the truth of the Gospel, keeping them bound in darkness and ignorance. This is why our call as believers is not just to see clearly but to act as beacons of light, illuminating the path for others to find their way to Christ.

Spiritual understanding is the key that unlocks the practical application of our spiritual vision. It involves more than just intellectual acknowledgment; it requires a deep, personal insight into the ways and will of God. Spiritual understanding allows us to navigate life's challenges with divine perspective, making decisions and taking actions that align with God's purposes.

Finally, it's important to understand that while physical sight is dependent on external light, spiritual vision requires the illumination of God's Word to function properly. Just as physical darkness renders physical sight useless, spiritual darkness can obscure our spiritual vision. However, when we are **born again**, our spirit is rejuvenated, and we gain the capacity to see with new eyes—eyes that perceive the spiritual realities hidden from our natural sight.

REFLECTIVE QUESTIONS

1. How does understanding spiritual vision change the way you view your challenges and opportunities?
2. In what ways can you actively seek to open your spiritual eyes to see God's hand in your life more clearly?
3. How has the concept of having two sets of eyes—one for the physical and one for the spiritual—helped you in your spiritual walk?
4. What steps can you take to ensure that your spiritual sight is being used to its full potential?
5. How can the story of Elisha and his servant inspire you to trust in God's protection and provision even when you cannot see it physically?

Actionable Steps

- **Cultivate a Visionary Mindset**: Start each day with a prayer that God would open your spiritual eyes to see His hand at work in your life and to perceive the opportunities He presents.
- **Equip with Knowledge**: Regularly study biblical examples of individuals who walked by faith and not by sight, such as Elisha and Paul, to understand how their spiritual vision guided their decisions and actions.
- **Engage in Spiritual Warfare**: Use the truths of God's Word as your weapon in battling the spiritual blindness that seeks to hinder your walk with Christ. Pray for the illumination of the Holy Spirit to reveal not just the realities of your circumstances but also the spiritual truths that govern them.

Journaling **Prompt**

Reflect on a time when you felt spiritually blind—unable to see God's plan in your circumstances. How did you seek clarity, and what was the outcome? Consider how your understanding of spiritual vision can transform your approach to similar situations in the future.

∾

WHAT IS VISION?

CHAPTER 3

ALIGNING YOUR VISION WITH THE TIMES

Be steadfast, immovable, always abounding in the work of the Lord, knowing that your labor is not in vain in the Lord. - 1 Corinthians 15:58 (NKJV)

In this chapter, we explore how imperative it is for us, as believers, to **develop God-sized visions** that bring faith, hope, and deliverance in a world that seems to be spiraling out of control. We are reminded that our calling in these trying times is not merely to survive but to thrive and enact divine changes. The Scriptures provide a firm foundation for this concept. As we read in Psalm 119:18, we ask God to "Unveil thou mine eyes, and I shall perceive wondrous things of thy law." This plea for revelation is crucial as it aligns our vision with the divine and reveals the **biblical foundation for vision**.

Reflecting on the wisdom of the past can also provide guidance for the present. The words of Shakespeare from *Julius Caesar*, "There is a tide in the affairs of men, which, taken at the flood, leads on to fortune," resonate deeply today. They illustrate the concept of **Shakespeare's insight on seizing opportunities**

—a call to action for us to grasp the crucial moments that life presents us. This aligns with our discussion on how **co-laboring with God** involves recognizing when God is moving and joining Him in that work. It's about understanding that God has a part that only He can fulfill, and there is a part that He expects us to do in order to bring His kingdom to fruition on earth.

One of the most practical steps in this journey is the act of writing down our visions. Habakkuk 2:2 says, "Write the vision, and make it plain on tablets, that he may run who reads it." This directive from God highlights the **importance of writing the vision**. It is not enough to simply have a vision; it must be documented. This ensures that the vision is clear and actionable, not just for ourselves but also for those who will join us in bringing it to pass. I learned this through personal experience when seeking a home with my wife. By **writing down specific details of what we desired**, we saw God's hand move miraculously, providing a home that met nearly all our specified criteria.

Our ability to harness and express our visions can often be enhanced by the wisdom of those who have gone before us. Peter Daniels, a successful entrepreneur, once shared insights that profoundly shaped my understanding of how **vision integrates with commitment and energy**. These elements are essential for giving life to our missions. Daniels emphasized that the dynamism of our vision is what fuels its realization, which brings us to the significance of a **mission statement**. At Church For All Nations, for example, our mission to empower locally and send globally forms the bedrock upon which all our visions are built. This underlines the importance of having a **clearly defined personal and corporate mission**.

Understanding the **enduring impact of vision** is also vital. What we do here on earth will echo into eternity. The things we build, the lives we touch, and the visions we fulfill have lasting implications beyond our temporal existence. This eternal perspective should motivate us to pursue our divine callings with even greater passion.

Navigating our journey requires a clear roadmap, and our vision acts like **God's Positioning System**. By setting clear goals and milestones, we can follow divine prompts and recalibrate whenever necessary, ensuring we remain on the path God has set for us. This metaphor highlights how **a vision must be specific and well-defined**, much like entering a precise location into a GPS.

Every vision is unique, tailored by God to fit the individual He has created. Just as our physical characteristics like fingerprints are unique to each of us, so is the vision God entrusts to us. Recognizing the **uniqueness of individual vision** helps us embrace and pursue our divine assignments with confidence and dedication.

In conclusion, understanding and aligning with our divine vision is not just about achieving personal goals—it's about fulfilling God's kingdom purposes on earth. As we continue to explore and articulate our visions, let's remain committed to the divine blueprint, knowing that each step forward is a step taken in partnership with God toward a legacy that lasts beyond our lifetime.

REFLECTIVE QUESTIONS

1. How does the current global climate influence your perception of the need for a personal vision?
2. What specific scriptures have you found that inspire you to pursue your God-given vision?
3. Reflect on a time when you seized an opportunity that felt divinely timed. What was the outcome?

4. How do you differentiate between your tasks and what you expect God to do in the process of realizing your vision?

5. In what ways can you better document and revisit the visions or goals you believe God has shown you?

ACTIONABLE STEPS

- **Cultivate a Habit of Visionary Thinking:** Regularly set aside time to read and meditate on scriptures related to vision and divine purpose. Use these sessions to ask God to clarify and renew your vision.
- **Equip Yourself with Tools for Documentation:** Invest in a journal or digital app specifically for recording insights, visions, and progress. This practice will help you keep track of divine inspirations and the fulfillment of God's promises.
- **Engage with a Community of Visionaries:** Seek out and join a group or community where visions and divine purposes are discussed and nurtured. Engaging with like-minded believers can provide encouragement and accountability.

JOURNALING Prompt

Reflect on the quote from Shakespeare used in the chapter and write about a current "tide in the affairs of men" in your life. How can you "take the current when it serves" to align your vision with God's timing and purposes?

_____

_____

_____

_____

_____

_____

_____

_____

_____

_____

_____

_____

_____

_____

_____

_____

_____

_____

_____

_____

_____

_____

_____

_____

_____

CHAPTER 4
HEAVENLY VISION THAT CONFRONTS THE GATES OF HELL

Do not be conformed to this world, but be transformed by the renewal of your mind, that by testing you may discern what is the will of God, what is good and acceptable and perfect. - Romans 12:2 (NKJV)

In this chapter, we delve into the profound necessity of adhering to a **Heavenly Vision that Confronts the Gates of Hell**, as inspired by Acts 16:19. This vision isn't born out of personal ambition or worldly desires but emerges from a divine revelation that deeply aligns with God's purposes. As believers, it is imperative that we do not walk in disobedience to this revelation, as it sets the course for a life that truly impacts the kingdom of God.

The essence of this vision is illuminated through **spiritual enlightenment**, as emphasized in Ephesians 1:18. This enlightenment, or the light of God flooding our hearts, allows us to see beyond the natural into the supernatural realm where God's will becomes clear. This understanding is crucial because without it, we wander aimlessly, blinded to the divine path set before us. Our role extends beyond personal salvation; we are to act as beacons of light in a world shrouded in darkness, reflecting God's truth and love to those lost in the shadows.

This concept of shining forth is further elaborated in Matthew 5:16, where we are urged to let our light shine before others that they may see our good works and glorify our Father in heaven. This instruction is part of our **role as believers in dispelling darkness**. Our lives, transformed and illuminated by God's presence, serve as living testimonies to His power and grace, drawing others towards Him.

However, the pursuit of this heavenly vision must transcend earthly desires, such as the accumulation of wealth or material possessions. While these things may indeed be added to us, as mentioned in the Scriptures, they should not distract or become idols. The **vision transcends material desires** and focuses on deeper, eternal priorities. It's about aligning our desires with God's kingdom and seeking His righteousness above all else, ensuring that our pursuits glorify Him and not ourselves.

The scope of God's plan for our lives is vast and intricately designed, far surpassing anything we could dream or imagine. In Psalm 139, we learn that God has crafted an opulent and detailed plan for each of us, a plan that **surpasses our own** limited understanding and expectations. By embracing this divine blueprint, we step into a life of greater fulfillment and purpose, one that aligns with God's overarching narrative of redemption and restoration.

Yet, as we journey towards fulfilling this vision, we must be constantly aware that we have an adversary. This adversary seeks to thwart our progress and disrupt the divine destiny set before us. Acknowledging this, our **awareness of spiritual opposition** becomes a crucial element of our spiritual walk. It compels us to lean not on our own strength but on the power and wisdom of God, who guides and protects us through every challenge.

Our approach to this vision requires a transformation of our mindset, adopting **higher ways of thinking and seeing** as outlined in Isaiah 55:8-9. By elevating our thoughts and perspectives to align with God's, we begin to understand His ways, which are higher than ours. This alignment is essential for navigating the complexities of our calling and for implementing the vision He has entrusted to us.

Understanding God's call is not merely about recognizing a divine assignment but is an ongoing **discovery process** of what we are meant to do. This process reveals the specific tasks and roles we are to play in the body of Christ. It involves a deep engagement with God's Word and a responsive obedience to His leading, ensuring that we are equipped for every good work He has prepared in advance for us.

Indeed, **God equips the called**. As we step into our calling, we can be confident that God will provide all that is necessary for us to fulfill His purposes. This equipping is comprehensive, encompassing every aspect of our being and ministry. As we develop the gifts and callings He has placed within us, we become more effective instruments in His hands, capable of carrying out His will on earth.

Lastly, our journey toward realizing the heavenly vision must be marked by **obedience and diligence**. Following this vision is not a passive endeavor; it demands active engagement and persistent effort. It requires us to immerse ourselves in the Scriptures, to live out the truths we discover, and to continually seek God's guidance. By doing so, we ensure that our path remains aligned with His will, enabling us to effectively confront and overcome the gates of hell.

Reflective Questions

1. How has your understanding of God's vision for your life changed after reading this chapter?
2. In what ways can you enhance your spiritual enlightenment to better discern God's purposes?
3. How do you reflect God's light in your everyday actions, especially in challenging situations?
4. What material desires might be hindering your pursuit of the heavenly vision?
5. Can you identify a time when you felt opposition in your spiritual journey? How did you handle it?

Actionable Steps

- **Cultivate Spiritual Discipline:** Dedicate time each day for prayer and meditation on the Scriptures. This routine will enhance your spiritual enlightenment and understanding of God's vision.
- **Equip Yourself with God's Word:** Engage deeply with the Bible through study and application. Utilize resources like commentaries, Bible studies, and teachings to gain a fuller understanding of the Scriptures.
- **Engage in Community and Service:** Actively participate in a community of faith where you can serve others and share the light of Christ. This involvement not only helps dispel darkness but also strengthens your own faith.

JOURNALING Prompt

Reflect on the current state of your spiritual vision. How clearly do you see God's plan for your life? What steps can you take to align more closely with the heavenly vision that confronts the gates of hell? Consider areas in your life where you might be walking in spiritual blindness and how you can invite God's light to illuminate those areas.

~

_____

_____

_____

_____

_____

_____

_____

_____

_____

_____

_____

_____

_____

_____

_____

_____

_____

_____

_____

_____

_____

_____

_____

_____

_____

_____

_____

_____

HEAVENLY VISION THAT CONFRONTS THE GATES OF HELL

THE POWER OF RIGHT THINKING

"Finally, brethren, whatever things are true, whatever things are noble, whatever things are just, whatever things are pure, whatever things are lovely, whatever things are of good report, if there is any virtue and if there is anything praiseworthy—meditate on these things." - Philippians 4:8 (NKJV)

In Chapter 5 of our journey, we delve into the profound impact of right thinking as guided by the profound scriptural principle: "For as he thinketh in his heart, so is he" from Proverbs 23:7. This scripture lays the foundation for understanding how integral our thoughts are to our identity and actions. It's essential to grasp that **Foundation in God's Image** means we were created not just to exist, but to thrive through the divine-like ability to create and influence our reality, which is expressed most vividly through our thoughts and imaginations.

We, as **Autonomy and Free Moral Agents**, have the inherent right to choose our paths. This freedom, a sacred gift from God, underscores the weight of responsibility on our shoulders to choose wisely and well. This decision-making power affects not only the course of our lives but also the lives of others around us, reflecting the profound moral responsibility entrusted to us by our Creator.

As we explore the depths of our minds, we discover that our **Imagination as a Battleground** is a primary field where spiritual warfare is waged. The forces that vie for control over our imagination are potent, for what occupies our minds can control our lives. The Apostle Paul's teachings in 2 Corinthians 10:3-5 clarify that our battles are not against flesh and blood but against these very forces that seek to corrupt and control our thoughts.

Guarding the Heart is not merely an ancient proverb but a vital strategy for spiritual and mental health. As the center of our emotional and spiritual life, the heart, much like fertile soil, can sprout either beneficial harvests or destructive weeds, depending on what seeds we allow to take root. This reality makes the vigilant monitoring of what we consume through media and conversations critically important.

Our daily actions are often dictated by the **Subconscious Influence and Habits** we develop. These habits form in the subconscious, driving our behaviors often without our conscious awareness, as illustrated by the automatic nature of driving a car. Recognizing and reforming these subconscious patterns are crucial to living a life aligned with God's will.

In today's culture, the **Cultural and Media Influence** is profound and pervasive, acting much like the farmer who sows seeds in the soil. Our minds, when left unguarded, can absorb both constructive and destructive ideas. This analogy calls for vigilant discernment, especially in today's media-saturated culture where negative influences are rampant.

The **Power of Imagination in Creation** is evident throughout history, where mere thoughts have given rise to innovations that have revolutionized societies. From the Wright brothers' first flight to the rapid advancements in technology, it is clear that what we can imagine, we can manifest into reality. This incredible capability reflects the divine spark within us, urging us to create and innovate in ways that honor God and serve humanity.

However, the potential of our thoughts means we must also master the art of **Taking Thoughts Captive**. Every thought that flits through our mind must be examined and brought into compliance with Christ's teachings. This process is crucial in maintaining spiritual integrity and ensuring that our thoughts contribute to our growth rather than our downfall.

Moreover, the **Impact of Positive vs. Negative Imagination** cannot be overstated. Our minds can cultivate visions of hope and prosperity or fear and destruction. The choice of nurturing positive, godly thoughts can lead to a life that embodies the fruit of the Spirit, whereas negative thoughts can spiral into destructive patterns.

Lastly, **Scriptural Meditation for Positive Thinking** provides a practical approach to cultivating a healthy mind. Philippians 4:8 serves as a guide for filtering our thoughts, urging us to focus on the noble, the pure, and the lovely. By meditating on these virtues, we align our minds with Christ's mind, fostering a mental environment conducive to spiritual growth and maturity.

REFLECTIVE QUESTIONS

1. How do you currently guard your heart and mind against negative influences?
2. What role does your imagination play in your daily decision-making?

3. Can you identify a habit that has been formed subconsciously but affects your spiritual walk?
4. How can you more effectively take every thought captive to the obedience of Christ?
5. Reflect on a time when a positive thought led to a positive outcome in your life. What was the situation?

ACTIONABLE STEPS

- **Cultivate a Positive Mental Environment:** Regularly engage in activities that promote positive thinking, such as reading uplifting literature, spending time in nature, or engaging in wholesome entertainment that aligns with biblical values.
- **Equip Yourself with Scripture:** Memorize and meditate on scriptures like Philippians 4:8. This will arm you with the necessary tools to combat negative thoughts and replace them with God-centered ones.
- **Engage in Community Accountability:** Regularly meet with a trusted group of fellow believers to discuss and hold each other accountable for maintaining a positive and biblically aligned thought life.

JOURNALING Prompt

Reflect on your daily thought patterns. Identify any recurring negative thoughts and consider their origins. How can you apply Philippians 4:8 to these thoughts to transform them into a positive mental framework?

~

CHAPTER 6

THE ROLE OF TESTING IN THE POWER OF VISION

"Count it all joy, my brothers, when you meet trials of various kinds, for you know that the testing of your faith produces steadfastness." - James 1:2-3 (NKJV)

I n Chapter 6, we explore the profound **Nature and Purpose of Testing**, an aspect of life that shapes and defines our spiritual journey. Tests are not merely obstacles; they are instruments of refinement, preparing us for greater things both in the natural and spiritual realms. When you begin to understand this, you can shift your perspective to welcome these times as opportunities for growth and preparation for promotion.

Differentiating between **tests, trials, and temptations** is crucial for any believer. Each serves a distinct purpose in our development: tests strengthen our faith, trials refine our character, and temptations, which are to be resisted, help us define our boundaries and commitments. Recognizing the type of challenge you are facing is key to handling it appropriately.

Testing Strengthens Faith in a way that is similar to how physical exercise strengthens the body. Just as resistance training builds muscle, spiritual tests build faith. James 1:3 tells us that the testing of our faith develops perseverance, which is essential for spiritual maturity. This growth is inevitable and necessary, akin to how a student learns through academic challenges.

Living in a fallen world, we are constantly swimming against a current of **worldly influence and spiritual resistance**. Like living fish that swim upstream, we must exert effort to live out our convictions. This effort is our testimony to the power of living faith that overcomes the world's darkness, as affirmed in John 1:5, where it is proclaimed that light always triumphs over darkness.

God's Sovereignty Over Temptation reminds us that while God tests us to improve and prepare us, He does not tempt us with evil. Understanding the origin of temptations helps us seek God's strength and wisdom to overcome them, as we are taught in James 1:13-14. This distinction is critical for maintaining our spiritual integrity and focus.

The application of these principles often comes to life in real-world scenarios, as I have shared in various sermons, drawing on **practical application of spiritual lessons** from my own experiences. For example, unexpected academic tests during my school days taught me the value of constant preparedness—a lesson directly applicable to spiritual readiness.

Reflecting on **Jesus as our example**, particularly during His trials in the wilderness and at Gethsemane, provides profound insights into the necessity of our tests and trials. Hebrews 5:7-8 intriguingly notes that even Jesus learned obedience through what He suffered. This highlights that if testing was necessary for the Son of God, how much more so for us?

The **role of Scripture in testing** cannot be overstated. The Word of God not only warns us of impending trials but also equips us with the wisdom to endure and overcome them.

Regular engagement with Scripture is akin to a student diligently studying to pass not just academic tests but life's tests.

Impact of Testing on Spiritual Maturity emphasizes that tests are not just challenges but opportunities for profound spiritual growth and maturity. They push us into deeper reliance on God, strengthening our spiritual resolve and enhancing our ability to navigate future challenges.

Finally, **Endurance Through Testing** is a call to persevere through challenges with a steadfast spirit. Knowing that these tests produce endurance, we can face them with confidence, encouraged by scriptures like James 1:2-3, which teach us to consider trials as pure joy because of the growth they bring.

As we conclude this chapter, let us embrace the tests and trials of life not as mere hardships but as opportunities to demonstrate the power of our vision and faith. Let these challenges be moments where we grow closer to realizing the full potential of what God has in store for us, armed with the knowledge that every test has a purpose and every trial has a reward.

REFLECTIVE QUESTIONS

1. How do you differentiate between a test, a trial, and a temptation in your own life?
2. Can you recall a time when a test or trial significantly strengthened your faith? What was the outcome?
3. How does understanding that Jesus was tested influence your response to your own tests?
4. What scriptures have helped you face tests and trials in your life?
5. How do you prepare yourself daily to face the tests and trials that may come?

. . .

ACTIONABLE STEPS

- **Cultivate a Routine of Prayer and Meditation:** Start each day with prayer and scripture reading to strengthen your spiritual foundations and prepare for any tests or trials that may arise.
- **Equip Yourself with Knowledge:** Regularly study the Bible to understand more deeply the nature of tests and how God uses them to develop character and faith.
- **Engage in Fellowship for Support:** Actively participate in a faith community where experiences and wisdom can be shared. This engagement provides both support and accountability during testing times.

JOURNALING Prompt

Reflect on the last significant test or trial you faced. How did you respond? What lessons did you learn, and how can you apply those lessons to future challenges? Consider how this has shaped your faith and what changes you might need to make to be better prepared for future tests.

∿

THE ROLE OF TESTING IN THE POWER OF VISION

_____

_____

_____

_____

_____

_____

_____

_____

_____

_____

_____

_____

_____

_____

_____

_____

_____

_____

_____

_____

_____

_____

_____

_____

_____

_____

_____

_____

CHAPTER 7

KINGDOM DISCIPLES RUNNING WITH THE HEAVENLY VISION

Let love be your highest goal! - 1 Corinthians 14:1 (NKJV)

I n Chapter 7, we explore the transformative power of living as Kingdom disciples, focusing on the heavenly vision of loving God and our neighbors with our whole being. This **Integration of Love for God and Neighbor** is foundational, illustrating that true adherence to the first commandment naturally leads to the fulfillment of the second. This seamless bond shows that to love our neighbors effectively, we must first be rooted in the love of God, as this love is poured into our hearts through the Holy Spirit.

The necessity of having **The Necessity of Divine Love** in our hearts is crucial because it empowers us to perform acts of love that are beyond our natural inclinations, such as blessing those who curse us. It's this divine love that enables us to see others through God's eyes, rather than our limited perspectives. Embracing this love ensures that our actions are aligned with God's will, rather than merely human empathy or willpower.

Prioritizing God in Our Lives sets the course for everything else. When we place God at the forefront of our lives, all other aspects follow suit, aligning under His governance and providence. This prioritization ensures that our pursuits are not just for personal gain but are aligned with building His kingdom. It's about seeking the kingdom of God and His righteousness first, which Jesus emphasized as the key to having all things added unto us.

Understanding our **Righteousness Through Christ** is transformative. It shifts our identity from one of sin and guilt to one of righteousness and acceptance, allowing us to stand before God without the weight of sin. This righteousness, gifted through Christ's sacrifice, is distinct from holiness, which pertains to our actions and behaviors—righteousness is about our standing with God, secured and unchanging.

The chapter also highlights the **Vision and Dreaming Inspired by God**, stressing that our spiritual vision and dreams are vital components of our journey with God. The enemy seeks to stifle these because they are powerful tools for our spiritual advancement and fulfillment of God's purposes. Thus, nurturing our capacity to dream within the realm of God's will is crucial for personal and communal spiritual growth.

In dealing with dreams and visions, **Distinguishing Between Spiritual Dreams and Nightmares** is essential. Not all dreams are from God; understanding this helps us discern and respond appropriately, whether that means rebuking a nightmare or embracing a divine revelation. This discernment is crucial for spiritual warfare, as it helps us to fight effectively against the enemy's schemes.

The Role of Dreams in Spiritual Warfare underscores that our dream life can be a battleground where spiritual victories or defeats can occur. Guarding our spiritual input, especially before sleep, is vital to ensuring that what we feed our minds does not become a foothold for the enemy. This guarding is part of our daily spiritual armor, keeping us aligned with God's truth and purposes.

The **Guarding Against Negative Influences** is particularly poignant in today's media-saturated culture. What we consume through media can seep into our dreams and subconscious, shaping our thoughts and attitudes in ways that may not align with God's word. Therefore, filling our minds with scriptural truth and godly content is essential to maintain spiritual purity and power.

The **Power of Consciously Dreamed Visions** and **The Importance of Intercession Based on Dreams** reflect the proactive and reactive aspects of spiritual visioning. Actively engaging in godly daydreaming can set the stage for divine inspiration, while being vigilant in intercession when God reveals specific needs or threats in dreams is crucial for spiritual warfare and protection.

This chapter invites you to embrace the comprehensive call of a Kingdom disciple, integrating deep love for God and neighbors with a life led by divine vision and dreams. As we explore these themes, we uncover the profound connection between our spiritual practices and the heavenly vision that guides us. Each point leads us back to the heart of our faith—living a life that transcends the ordinary and impacts the eternal.

REFLECTIVE QUESTIONS

1. How do you practice loving God with all aspects of your being in daily life?
2. In what ways have you experienced the power of God's love in difficult relational moments?
3. How do you discern and guard against negative spiritual influences in your life?

4. What role do dreams play in your spiritual life and how do you respond to them?
5. How has understanding your righteousness in Christ affected your spiritual confidence and actions?

ACTIONABLE STEPS

- **Cultivate a Heart of Worship:** Dedicate time daily to worship and prayer, focusing on deepening your love and commitment to God. This practice strengthens your spiritual foundation and prepares you for loving service.
- **Equip Yourself with Scriptural Truths:** Regularly study scriptures related to God's love, righteousness, and the power of vision. This knowledge will help you live out your faith confidently and with a clear understanding of your identity in Christ.
- **Engage in Community and Service:** Actively participate in community service and church activities that allow you to practice loving your neighbor as yourself. These activities not only foster personal growth but also build the kingdom of God in tangible ways.

JOURNALING Prompt

Reflect on how the integration of loving God and your neighbor has influenced your personal spiritual journey. How can you further develop this love in your daily life to align more closely with the heavenly vision?

CHAPTER 8

AMERICA: A MODERN-DAY MANIFESTATION OF THE HEAVENLY VISION

There is no greater call than to walk in the light of God's vision. For America, the heavenly vision is not just a historic concept but a present and living reality. The founding of this nation was built on biblical principles, and as long as we align with God's Word, we will see His glory shine through this land. It is not too late to reclaim the vision God has for us—personally, as communities, and as a nation. God's plans for America are not finished. In fact, we have a divine responsibility to steward the blessings He has poured upon us for the advancement of His Kingdom. Though challenges surround us, we must hold fast to the truth that light always overcomes darkness, and we are called to be that light in this world.

"Righteousness exalts a nation, but sin is a reproach to any people." —Proverbs 14:34 NKJV

The **foundation of America's vision is in its reliance on God's Word.** When the Liberty Bell was inscribed with "Proclaim Liberty Throughout All the Land

Unto All the Inhabitants thereof" from Leviticus 25:10, it symbolized the biblical roots of America's freedoms. Without the Bible, this nation would never have existed, and the blessings we have enjoyed for centuries would not have been possible. Yet today, **tyranny threatens the heavenly vision** entrusted to us. From government overreach to the erosion of family values, we see the effects of sin and compromise. The warnings of 2 Timothy 3:1 have become reality, as perilous times now manifest before our eyes. It is a sobering reminder that God will not be mocked—our obedience determines the future of this nation.

Divine providence was key to America's success, as our founding fathers knew. In their fight for independence, they declared their "firm reliance on the protection of Divine Providence." The hand of God guided them to craft a government that would protect liberty and freedom, but **Christian principles are America's cornerstone.** The founders were clear that faith in Christ and adherence to His Word were essential for sustaining this nation. John Adams boldly stated that the principles of Christianity were the foundation of America's independence. As Andrew Jackson proclaimed, the Bible is "the Rock upon which our republic rests." These truths remind us that without righteousness, no nation can stand.

Our **responsibility for America's blessings** cannot be overstated. Luke 12:48 declares that "to whom much is given, much will be required." America's prosperity and freedoms are not just privileges—they are responsibilities that demand faithful stewardship. Unfortunately, **spiritual decline has left America vulnerable,** as material comfort has led to spiritual complacency. This spiritual weakness has opened the door to tyranny and moral decay. But God, in His mercy, uses these times of testing to refine His people. **Testing refines and separates God's people,** as we witnessed during the COVID crisis. It was a season of sifting that revealed both faithfulness and compromise, separating the wheat from the tares.

Despite these challenges, **America as a manifestation of the heavenly vision** remains God's intention. John Adams called America's founding "a grand design in Providence for the illumination of mankind." America's purpose has always been to be a blessing to the nations and a light for the Gospel. This mission reminds us that **righteousness exalts a nation**, as Proverbs 14:34 states, while sin brings destruction. If America is to fulfill her destiny, we must return to the faith and righteousness of our founders. **The Great Commission is America's destiny**, as demonstrated from the very beginning. In 1607, the first settlers planted a cross on Virginia Beach and dedicated this land to the glory of God, praying that future generations would carry the Gospel to the ends of the earth. That prayer still stands today.

We must remember that **light always overcomes darkness**. No matter how fierce the opposition, the light of God's truth cannot be extinguished. Our responsibility is to let that light shine, just as our founders did. John Hancock's words remind us of our duty: "Resistance to tyranny becomes the Christian and social duty of each individual." If God is for us, no enemy can prevail. **We are called to stand and fight for God's vision**, refusing to be swayed by fear or compromise. America's strength lies not in her wealth or power but in her obedience to God. When we seek first His Kingdom and righteousness, we align ourselves with His heavenly vision.

Finally, I am reminded of Patrick Henry's declaration: "Guard with jealous attention the public liberty. Suspect everyone who approaches that jewel." His most cherished possession was his faith in Jesus Christ because he knew that true happiness and purpose can only be found in Him. Let us return to our foundation, remembering that God's plans for America are not finished.

By embracing the power of vision and walking in the light of God's Word, we will see His purposes fulfilled in this nation.

REFLECTIVE QUESTIONS

1. What role do biblical principles play in the foundation of America, and how can we apply them today?
2. How can testing and adversity strengthen your faith and refine your character in the midst of challenges?
3. What are some practical ways you can stand against tyranny and uphold God's truth in your community?
4. Why is it essential to recognize that blessings come with responsibility, especially in light of America's prosperity?
5. How can you personally contribute to fulfilling the Great Commission and advancing God's heavenly vision for your nation?

ACTIONABLE STEPS

- **Cultivate: Deepen your understanding of America's Christian heritage** by studying the biblical foundations of the nation's founding and reflecting on how faith influenced the lives of the early leaders.
- **Equip: Prepare yourself spiritually and mentally** to stand firm in your faith during times of testing. Commit to daily prayer, Bible study, and worship to strengthen your reliance on God's Word.

- **Engage: Take a bold stand for righteousness** in your community by speaking up for truth, participating in godly initiatives, and supporting leaders who align with biblical values.

JOURNALING **Prompt**

Reflect on the statement, "Righteousness exalts a nation, but sin is a reproach to any people" (Proverbs 14:34 NKJV). Write about specific ways you can seek righteousness in your own life and how that pursuit can influence your family, church, and nation. How can you align yourself with God's heavenly vision for America today?

∼

Harrison House

Harrison House is a Spirit-filled, Word of Faith Christian publisher dedicated to spreading the message of faith, hope, and love through our wide range of inspiring publications. Committed to the messages that highlight the power of the Word and Spirit, we provide books, devotionals, and study guides that empower believers to live victorious, faith-filled lives.

Our resources are designed to help readers grow spiritually, strengthen their faith, and experience the transformative power of God's Word. Harrison House is passionate about equipping Christians with the tools they need to fulfill their divine purpose and impact the world for Christ.

www.ingramcontent.com/pod-product-compliance
Lightning Source LLC
Chambersburg PA
CBHW060428090426
42734CB00011B/2485